Let the miracles
begin...

THE

GRATITUDE
JAR

A SIMPLE GUIDE
TO CREATING MIRACLES

JOSIE ROBINSON

ISBN 13: 978-1-940014-46-3
eISBN 13: 978-1-940014-47-0
Library of Congress Number: 2014955922
Printed in Canada

20 19 18 17 16   6 5 4 3 2

Cover design by Jessie Sayward Bright
Book Design by Ryan Scheife / Mayfly Design
Typeset in the Quadraat, Myriad Pro, and Trend Sans typefaces

Published by Wise Ink Creative Publishing
Minneapolis, Minnesota
www.wiseinkpub.com

To order, visit www.itascabooks.com or call 1-800-901-3480.
Reseller discounts available.

If the only prayer you say in your life is "thank you,"
that would suffice.

—MEISTER ECKHART

Lucas: Do you know what, Mommy?
Me: What?
Lucas: I appreciate my life. I really, really, really do.

—LUCAS, MY FOUR-YEAR-OLD,
TWO WEEKS AFTER USING
THE GRATITUDE JAR FOR THE FIRST TIME

CONTENTS

Gratitude (*noun*): The state of being grateful; thankfulness. The quality of being thankful; readiness to show appreciation for and to return kindness.

Synonyms: Gratefulness – appreciation – thankfulness – thanks

THE RABBI AND THE SECRET NAME OF GOD

"Gratitude is not only the greatest of virtues, but the parent of all others."

—Cicero

There once was a rabbi so wise and devout that he was considered a saint. God had blessed this rabbi with knowledge no other human possessed. Rumors spread that the rabbi even knew the most secret name of God, a name so holy that whoever said it aloud could perform any miracle they wished. However, there was a catch: whoever said this secret name of God would never achieve salvation because the name was so holy that it wasn't to be uttered by man.

One day, a sick man was brought to the rabbi for healing. This man was so ill, the rabbi realized while the man was waiting to see him, that he was already on the brink of death. It was too late; the victim would die before any healing could occur. The rabbi felt hopeless.

At that moment, in pure desperation, the rabbi raised his head to heaven and cried out to God using the secret, forbidden name to heal the dying man.

Miraculously, the man opened his eyes and asked for a drink of water and some food. He thanked the rabbi profusely for the miracle that had just been performed. The man explained to the family gathered around that he had seen the gates of heaven open to welcome him but had heard the rabbi's voice calling him back to life. He had been brought back from the dead. It was a true miracle.

The rabbi's disciples stood by and watched with disbelief. They couldn't believe their teacher had given up salvation by speaking the forbidden name aloud! The disciples became even more shocked when the rabbi started jumping up and down with glee, giving praise to God.

"How can you rejoice, when you have just given up all hope for your own salvation?" they asked.

The rabbi stopped. "Don't you see? Don't you understand? Finally, I know I serve God because I love Him, not because I hope to get something in return."

He continued, "The last doubt has finally vanished, the doubt I have for my own motives. I now know my love for God isn't motivated by greed, but by pure love without desire for personal gain."

"*Rejoice with me, my friends, for I am free of myself at last.*"

—JEWISH PARABLE

CHAPTER ONE

BEFORE GRATITUDE

"There are only two ways to live your life. One is as though nothing is a miracle. The other is as though everything is a miracle."

—ALBERT EINSTEIN

When the student is ready, the teacher appears. Mine found me during a snowy Minnesota February when I was a disenchanted housewife with a big drinking problem. So it was a good thing she found me when she did. My teacher introduced me to the Gratitude Jar—the thing that ultimately turned my life into a miracle.

At the time, my husband, Shawn, and I were living in a little rambler with our two boys, ages four and almost one. My husband worked as a high school English teacher. I was a stay-at-home mom and *very* part-time school counselor. Over the years, my part-time position had been cut to almost nothing, so I just used it as an excuse to stay home with the kids. We made it work as best we could and scraped by month-to-month on my husband's teacher salary.

On the surface, it had all the makings of a quaint life: mom at home with the kids, dad off to work. Me making homemade meals from scratch (much cheaper) and going on fun, free field trips around the city. Most of my mom friends worked full-time and frequently told me how much they envied me. *How great to be home all day! You must be so happy!*

Yes, I love it, I'd say, smiling. Then I'd launch into a story about a silly tea party the boys and I just had or some crazy outdoor adventure in our backyard. *I so love being a mom,* I'd say, smiling again.

But really, I was lying.

    It feels terrible to admit because I love my boys, my husband included, very much, but every morning when I awoke there was a knot of dread in my stomach about the day ahead. The constant laundry. Cleaning food particles off furniture. Trying to pretend I liked playing with cars and Star Wars figures. Diapers. Screaming. Whining. Being so broke that I didn't know how we were going to buy groceries for the week. Spending the baby's nap time making homemade whatever to make our food budget stretch as far as possible.

I hated it.

Most of all, I hated the fact that I hated it.

I was irritated, tense, or depressed almost always. Relief didn't arrive until my husband came home from work and I could *finally* start drinking around five p.m. I'd tell everyone it was time for me to start "working on dinner," which actually meant sneaking off to the kitchen to get loaded while taking a suspiciously long time to put together spaghetti and meatballs.

I felt good after my first glass of wine. After an entire bottle—and on most nights I had two—I didn't feel anything. I found numbness preferable to the near-constant irritation I felt all day. I'd then pass out on our oversized family room sofa while watching television, wake up the next morning with a giant hangover, and repeat the process all over again.

This cycle had been going on for several years. It started shortly after Lucas, my first child, was born. My husband said I went into a postpartum black hole right after delivery.

I think that's a pretty accurate description of what happened.

☞ Both mental illness and alcoholism run rampant in my family. I spent the early part of my life sneaking heavy pours and trying to prove that I wasn't crazy, too.

To prove this, I held everything in and presented

a perfectly controlled, pleasant image to the world. If something bothered me, it was squashed immediately. And I would go on with my life with a gigantic smile plastered to my face, telling everyone how great I was. I eventually became a counselor because I wanted to help people solve their problems, since I didn't have any of my own. I was great!

Nevertheless, there were a few red flags along the way. The first being that I was, in fact, mentally ill (I'd been diagnosed with an anxiety disorder in college). And the second being that I was also, in fact, an alcoholic (I used it to manage my anxiety and party like a rock star!). Despite efforts to the contrary, my apple didn't fall that far from the family tree.

Before Lucas was born, I was able to keep both these ugly facts about myself a secret because of how much work I put into my cheerful (!) and joyful (!) exterior. However, shortly after his delivery, when I was too damn tired and hormonal to keep anything in anymore, my crap came out, so to speak.

Imagine what happens to a can of soda when you shake it like crazy and pop off the top. The liquid explodes all over the place. That's what happened to me after I gave birth—I spewed all over the place. Emotionally.

I'd spent my whole life repressing, shaking it up, keeping it in, and repressing some more, all with a gigantic smile plastered to my face. I had so much emotion bottled inside of me that it was no wonder it all came gushing out with Lucas. I mean, it had to go somewhere.

In summary, I went nuts after becoming a mother.

෴ I stumbled along for several years, dealing with my spewing emotions while taking care of my new baby as best I could. Many nights Shawn came home to find me in Lucas's nursery, sitting in the rocking chair and bawling hysterically while Lucas slept peacefully in his crib. I never had a specific reason why I was crying; I just knew that I needed to.

Things got a little better as Lucas got older. My crying spells came less and less, and my panic attacks went from daily to monthly. I felt well enough to have another baby, Davis, almost four years after Lucas was born. I wasn't spewing emotionally anymore, but I still felt anxious and mildly depressed most of the time. About what, who knew. I just knew I didn't feel *good*, so I turned to my friend alcohol to cope.

Over the years, my drinking had gone from weekly social binge-drinking to daily problem-drinking. Alcohol was the thing I used to deal with my unpleasant emotions and numbed me from the overall dissatisfaction I felt with life. Frankly, it was the only thing I looked forward to each day. No, not spending time with my husband or children, but being alone with my bottle of red wine or tumbler of whiskey. Alcohol was my one and only favorite pastime.

My husband kept encouraging me to see a therapist since I was obviously not well, but I resisted. I was a counselor, dammit. I help people with *their* problems, not the other way around. No, I was going to figure this out on my own; I was going to help *myself*. Plus, I argued, we didn't have the money for me to go to therapy anyway. *I'll deal with it when the kids get older.*

Side note: I'm pathologically stubborn.

Even though things were better for a little while, meaning I could hold it together enough to manage my day-to-day activities, things eventually got worse. Which is what usually happens if you use alcohol to deal with your problems. When Lucas was four and a half and Davis still an infant, I hit bottom.

It happened at a close friend's surprise birthday party where I'd gotten shamefully drunk. I made a complete embarrassment out of myself that evening: slurring my way through small talk, shouting obscenities at the host of the party, stumbling over furniture. That night, several of my friends confronted me about my drinking and how it was out of control. They were worried about me. Was I okay? I didn't seem okay.

On most nights, I would've just reassured myself that my friends were wet blankets about my partying. Others had confronted me about it several times before, namely my husband, who I never listened to because

I considered him a nondrinking square whose opinion didn't count. But on that night, my denial blinders finally came off and I saw what everyone else was seeing: I was out of control and miserable.

When I woke up the next morning, feeling ill from all the drinking the night before, I knew I needed to change. I was so disconnected even though I had so much to live for: an amazing family, wonderful friends, good health, and on and on. I had it so good, but I just couldn't get out of my black hole to enjoy it.

That was my lowest point. My rock bottom. I stared at my bedroom ceiling a long time and cried. I really hated myself and started thinking my boys deserved better than drunk, bitchy, depressed me as their mother. I completely would have understood if they wanted to trade me in for a brand-new, nicer mom who would love them better.

I'd failed miserably at life.

I decided I needed an intervention.

So I rolled out of bed, dropped to my knees, and for the first time in over a decade—I prayed.

Hey, God! I know it's been a really long time since we last talked—sorry about that. How are you? Good. Okay. (FYI: I like to keep my prayers conversational.)

I need your help. But you probably knew that already, right? Right.

Okay, so I need you in my life. I'm ready to give my life to you.

I don't know what it is I need you to do, but I need you to do something.

Please help me. Please, please, please!

Just take it over. Everything. I can't live like this anymore, and I need you to live through me. Please bring me whatever serves my highest and best purpose.

Hit it, God. I'm ready.

Thanks.

Tell Jesus hi for me.

Love you.

Amen.

And that was it.

It wasn't one of those earth-shattering prayers you read about in Alcoholics Anonymous books, but it was sincere. I really, truly meant it. I got up, not feeling any different, still hungover, and walked into baby Davis's nursery to get him ready for the day.

Looking back on it, though, that prayer was my turning point. Because three days after I said it, I met Maleah.

My teacher.

CHAPTER TWO

THE TEACHER

"Just an observation: it is impossible to be both grateful and depressed.
Those with a grateful mindset tend to see the message in the mess. And
even though life may knock them down, the grateful find reasons, if even
small ones, to get up."

—STEVE MARABOLI, LIFE, THE TRUTH, AND BEING FREE

M aleah Jacobs is an intuitive from Seattle who
provides spiritual guidance and healing. (I
never expected God to answer my prayer
through a psychic, but clearly I needed all the help I
could get. Plus, it was free.) I met Maleah through my
sister-in-law, Emma, who had been hired to do advertis-
ing work for Maleah's busy Seattle practice.

When Emma flew home to Minnesota for a Christmas visit, I asked her what it was like working for a psychic because, honestly, I was fascinated. I'd always been

interested in that kind of thing but never had any first-hand experience with people who had those kinds of abilities. I wanted to learn more.

Emma told me Maleah's abilities were completely real and she'd given Emma information about her no one could possibly know. She also said she'd had several life-changing healing sessions with Maleah and encouraged me to purchase one for myself since it had been such a positive experience.

Seeing a spiritual healer was something I'd always been curious about, and I was definitely in a place where I needed a healing of some kind. Yet even though I wanted to, I couldn't afford it. No way could I indulge on such a luxury living on one income. Plus, I didn't know if I wanted someone peeking around my inner workings like that. I mean, who knew what she would find in there?

Emma, being the persistent, knowing sister that she is, bought me a session with Maleah that year for my Christmas present. Even though I was incredibly nervous to find out what this psychic healer was going to tell me, I went ahead and scheduled an appointment with Maleah near the end of January.

My first session happened to occur only three days after I'd went on my knees and prayed for an intervention. I didn't realize it until much later, but God had just answered my prayer.

⌒๑ "So here's what you've been doing. You're like, 'I'm Josie, I got this. No, it's cool. I got this. I got it. No, it's cool, I totally got it. It's cool, it's cool, it's cool.' But really," Maleah lowered her voice, "you so don't have it. You don't. You just don't. You need help."

She sighed and changed direction. "What are the kids I see around you? Do you have kids?"

"Yes. I have two boys," I said.

"They're little ones, right?"

"Yeah, they're four and eight months."

Maleah laughed. "Yeah, those are little ones, all right." She lowered her voice again. "So you're totally overwhelmed."

I nodded, which I found myself doing the entire course of our phone session together. It was uncanny how much this lady knew about me—things I'd never told anyone, not even my husband and especially not Emma—so any doubts I had about Maleah's psychic ability disappeared within the first few minutes of our conversation.

She continued, "The one thing you have control over is Josie. You have to ask and then receive. And you get to be an excellent, joyous receiver. You've got to not only ask for help, but you've also got to be on the lookout for *receiving* help."

I nodded again. I was terrible at both asking for and receiving help. A lot of the session focused on this issue and how I could get better—especially about asking my husband Shawn for it. "Shawn is just standing there, begging you to let him in, and you feel like you're not deserving of that support," she pointed out. "You grew up not knowing how. You were taught you had to be scrappy and do it all yourself, so that's what you're still doing."

Maleah continued, "But now you're a mother and a wife. You need help. That's your family. You can't be an island. I mean, some of the loneliest of us are in marriages and surrounded by friends and family. You're in this situation where you're feeling totally overwhelmed. So you get to give Shawn a list of things you need help with and then cry, and let him hold you while you cry." She stopped. "Oh my gosh, I see you rolling your eyes right now," she said with a laugh.

I was. I laughed along with her and tried to be more open to what she said even though I'm not a hold-me-while-I-cry type of person. She went on, "But that's going to make him feel more like a man, and he needs to know that you need him. So the first thing that needs to happen is *you* need to know that you need him."

I sighed. "Right, right." My husband is one of those eternally giving, generous people who would help anyone, anytime. But I was so darn stubborn about doing everything myself. I promised her I would get better about asking him for support from there on out. And maybe I'd let him hold me once in a while. Maybe.

Maleah explained, "Just let people do for you in the

way that they can do for you. You're depriving them of the opportunity to help you. You need to be specific and write down exactly what you want help with.

"The other thing I'm seeing right now is the laundry. What is up with your laundry situation? You need help with that."

I laughed aloud—I couldn't believe she picked up on that. I'd only ever told Shawn of my laundry hatred. Sometimes it felt like all I ever did was the bleeping laundry. "It's like the bane of my existence," I told her.

Maleah laughed. "I know. You feel like a laundry wench."

"It's so funny you said the thing about the laundry. I really can't believe it," I said, shaking my head.

"So decide to do it differently," she instructed. "Crank up some music, put on some earphones, and zone out. Pick some eighties hits. Pick some anthems. Do whatever you need to do to make it fun so that you can go somewhere else in your head while you do the laundry because it is your *good pleasure* to do the laundry."

She explained, "How you do anything is how you do everything. So if you do your laundry this way, you're going to do everything else in your life this way."

I sighed. "You're probably right. I'll work on it. I like the music idea. I think I could do that."

Maleah went on to give some suggestions for making things easier and other insights into how I could change my dysfunctional ways. Near the end of our session, she asked if I wanted to schedule another since much more healing still needed to occur.

I told her no, explaining how dead broke I was and that I couldn't afford to pay her for it. But I thanked her for the amazingness that was my one, and probably only, session.

Sensing I could still use some help since, let's face it, she's a psychic and can pick up on that stuff, Maleah generously offered one final session for basically free. I declined again, telling her I couldn't possibly without paying her, to which she gently reminded me I needed to work on receiving help and this was a direct example of me refusing it.

Right. So I said yes and scheduled another session for the next month.

In the meantime, I promised to work on some of the things we talked about: asking for help and, most importantly, receiving it. *Receiving it joyously*, as she said.

Also, organizing my life a bit better so I didn't feel so overwhelmed all the time. And of course, quitting all the drinking.

I felt a lot better afterwards. But I wasn't quite 100 percent yet—that didn't happen until after my next, and final, session with Maleah.

The session where I learned about the Gratitude Jar.

CHAPTER THREE

THE GRATITUDE JAR

"Gratitude can transform common days into thanksgivings, turn routine jobs into joy, and change ordinary opportunities into blessings."

—WILLIAM ARTHUR WARD

In the month that passed between sessions with Maleah, things improved dramatically.

I quit drinking completely, thanks to a little book written by Allen Carr called *The Easy Way to Quit Drinking* that found its way into my life around that time. The title said it all—the book made it easy for me to quit drinking. Don't ask me how or why it worked, but it did, amazingly. I've lost count of how many months I've been sober now (Part II of my prayer being answered. Thanks, God. And thanks to the late Allen Carr for writing the book).

I was also using a few of the techniques Maleah suggested for dealing with what I considered the drudgery of my life: laundry and perpetually picking up the house. I took her suggestion of putting music on in the background to make the chores more enjoyable. Surprisingly, this little trick worked and I found myself having a much better time doing these formerly dreaded chores of mine.

Maleah said how you do anything is how you do everything—including laundry. I found this to be true. I went from feeling resentful and irritated about doing my drudgery—to actually looking forward to it. I had *fun* picking up Storm Trooper helmets and Cheerios off the floor and folding laundry as long as my favorite eighties anthems were blasting in the background.

Maleah was also right that once I had fun in that part of my life, then I'd start having fun other places as well. I was playing with my kids and laughing with my husband more. It felt good to have a genuine smile on my face instead of the fake one I used to wear. I also felt better physically since I wasn't drinking so much alcohol anymore; I had more energy, and I felt emotionally stable and clear-headed. I realized drinking had been a huge cause of my moodiness.

My anxiety had also decreased. I wasn't feeling as overwhelmed since I had become better about asking for help. Shawn and I were in a much better place because of my newfound willingness to ask him for support; he enjoyed being wanted and needed, and I quit feeling so resentful toward him. I hadn't asked him to hold me yet, but I was getting there.

So when Maleah called for my next session, things were looking up. In fact, I was feeling better than I'd felt in a long time.

༶⁓ "The biggest thing that resonated with me from our last session was how checked out I was from Shawn," I said. "That's what bugged me the most. I realized when I get really stressed I get resentful toward him because I feel like I'm doing too many things and he's not helping me—even though I'm not asking him for any help. I end up pushing him away."

I continued, "And I was trying to do all this crap all the time. Like, get everything done every day, which was just dumb. So I came up with this schedule of doing laundry one day a week, let it all pile up, whatever, and do it in one day instead of a little every day. Turn my music on when I do it. Instead of trying to do everything every day, which is what I was doing before. It was maddening.

"And now, especially when I do it to music, I realize that stuff isn't even that bad. I don't mind doing it. I feel like my life is in a different place than it was a month ago, to be honest."

Maleah laughed. "Well, that's what all my pages of notes say, so let's keep going through the notes." She continued, "The next thing I wrote was: there are miracles all around you, and now you have the eyes to see them. That's awesome! Bless it."

I smiled and nodded. "Yes, I will. Definitely."

Maleah started, "So, the blessing thing, it's a practice. Now you have the eyes to see, and you need to know when you're in your Small Self and when you're in your Big Self. When you're in that Higher Self energy—you've been in that space now. You know when you're happy, joyous, free, peaceful, and useful. You know effortlessness and ease. It's a process. And you know what?" she whispered. "It's just going to get better."

I laughed. "That's good to know!"

Maleah continued, "You just have to get out of your own way, sweetsies, because even I don't know how good it's gonna get for you. I need to get out of the way too so the Universe can outdo both of us."

⌒ Maleah and I talked through some other things, mainly about the good stuff happening in my life at the moment. As we neared the end of our last session together, she asked if I was writing all these good things down. I said no, I wasn't. She suggested I start keeping a gratitude journal to document and give thanks for all these positive things.

Full disclosure: I'm not a journal person. When I hear the word "journal," it sounds like a lot of work I don't want to do. Even though I enjoy writing, I do not enjoy journaling. I think it stems from all the journals I had to write in eighth-grade English class or something.

22

I wasn't into it even though it sounded like a cool and productive idea.

Maleah sensed I wasn't feeling it too. "Okay, well another thing you could try is to put down all your blessings, all your wins, all your synchronicities on little slips of paper and put them in a jar."

That sounded okay; a jar was less work than a journal in my mind. "I like that. I think I could do that, probably."

"So do that. So on your yin days when you're like, ugh, I'm not feeling it, because those days are going to happen, you can pull those things out of your jar to remind yourself that yes, things are awesome! The Universe is constantly conspiring for my highest and best good always, always, always. I am outrageously supported.

"Can you do that? That sounds like fun, right?" It sounded like she still sensed my hesitation about the journal idea.

"That sounds like fun," I reassured her. "The journal didn't sound like fun, but the jar sounds like fun. I could do the jar."

"Right. So we're in agreement: you find a cool little jar, or a can, and decorate it if you want. And then you can put little scraps of paper in it as you notice blessings and gifts. A little gratitude something or just a win."

I thought about another way I could use the jar, because even though things were going well for me at the time, I still had a long way to go. I had fixed a lot of things in my life, gotten more organized, and quit the drinking, and I was better at asking for help from my husband, but I still felt disconnected from my children, especially my oldest son, Lucas.

Lucas and I hadn't spent much quality time together since his baby brother had been born, and I'd been in a black hole for so long—I needed a way to reconnect with him. I thought this might be a good way to do it, so I told Maleah, "This is something I think my oldest son would enjoy, too. I think I'll have him do it with me."

Maleah was silent for a long time and then slowly said, "That's brilliant."

She continued, "You know what, Josie? I would like you to entertain the idea of doing a Gratitude Jar with your four-year-old for the next thirty days. Record your conversations, and then I'd like you to write about it."

I nodded. "That'd be cool. I think I will do that."

"What's your four-year-old's name?" she asked.

"Lucas. His name is Lucas."

Maleah sighed. "Bless the mind of a four-year-old. This is going to be incredible."

She was right.

CHAPTER FOUR

THIRTY DAYS OF GRATITUDE WITH A FOUR-YEAR-OLD

"At times our own light goes out and is rekindled by a spark from another person. Each of us has cause to think with deep gratitude of those who have lighted the flame within us."

—ALBERT SCHWEITZER

"Test, test." I held the digital recorder to my mouth. Lucas looked at me quizzically.

"What are you doing, Mommy?"

"I'm going to record what we talk about tonight. We're going to say what we're thankful for, every night, for the next thirty days, and I'm going to record it with this." I waved the recorder in front of him.

Lucas and I were lying in his twin bed, getting ready for bedtime. He was in his Batman pajamas, snuggled under a fleece blanket. Sitting on the bed between us was our "Gratitude Jar."

I put it in air quotes because the closest thing to a jar I could find was a Star Wars Easter basket collecting dust in our storage room. I wrote THANK YOU with black Sharpie on a Post-It note and stuck it to the side of the basket. It was a little less classy than I'd envisioned, but it worked.

I pointed to the basket. "This is our Gratitude Jar, or thank you basket, I should say, so that you understand. Gratitude means thank you. So every night we're going to say—"

Lucas started pointing at the Star Wars characters on the basket. "I like it because of all the Star Wars guys, Anakin, Yoda, and the clones. I really like the clones."

"I know, they're pretty cool. So every night we're going to say—" Lucas interrupted again with a serious expression on his face. "They have armor, you know. The clones."

"I know." I'm familiar with all things Star Wars, but we needed to get on track. "We're going to say what we're thankful for. Okay?"

"Why?"

This was his favorite question of the moment for everything. "Because it's fun. It will help us think of all the good things we have in our life. It's nice to say thanks."

I took a deep breath. "This is a new thing mommy is trying out, okay? So do you want me to go first, or do you want to go first?"

"You first."

"Okay. I'm really thankful for my beautiful family." I smiled at him. "For you, for baby Davis, for Daddy, and our kitty, Mino. What are you thankful for, Lucas?"

He thought it over a few minutes and then said, "My baby brother and my dad and my mom." He leaned over and kissed my knee.

"Aw, I love you sweetie. Thank you." I leaned over and kissed his forehead in return.

Lucas pulled away and started again, "And I'm thankful for my G-Ma [his nickname for his grandmother Lori] too. That's all." He nodded his head matter-of-factly.

"That's all for tonight?"

"That's all." Lucas lied down and pulled up his blanket. He gave me a look that said, *It's time for bed, Mom. Let's wrap this up.* I took the hint.

"All right." I wrote our gratitudes on a few slips of paper, dropped them into the Star Wars basket, and placed it on his nightstand. "Good night, sweetie."

"Good night, Mommy."

☙ The next morning I woke up and stared at the ceiling like usual, thinking about the day ahead. My familiar knot of dread was still there but not as debilitating as it had been a few months ago. I heard the bedroom door open; Lucas ran in and jumped onto my bed. He snuggled up next to me and whispered in my ear, "Do you know what I'm thankful for, Mommy? My blankie. Are we going to do the thank you again tonight? I like it."

☙ As the week passed, Lucas and I continued our nightly Gratitude Jar routine. We didn't have much trouble coming up with new things. For Lucas, it was usually what he saw in front of him: stuffed animals, his blankie, the posters in his room. For me, it was also the things right in front of me—but that I had never noticed before, things like food, the sun, our house, my health.

Lucas Day Three: "I'm thankful for my nice warm, comfy bed I sleep in every night. It keeps me really cozy. And sometimes I get cold, but I have a blanket."

Mom Day Four: "I went grocery shopping today and I bought a lot of food and I'm thankful that we have a lot of food to feed our bellies and keep ourselves healthy."

Lucas Day Six: "I'm thankful for my room because it keeps me really warm. At playtime I get cold, so I put on sweatshirts. Then I take them off and I feel just right because I've been playing for a really long time."

Mom Day Six: "Do you know how you're learning about your senses in preschool right now?" Lucas nodded. "I'm thankful I have all of mine—that I can see, hear, taste, smell, and touch. It helps me enjoy my life so much more."

Mom Day Seven: "I'm thankful for the sun. I missed it today. It wasn't out."

"It was just out, like peeking out, three times today," Lucas observed.

"Yes, just a couple times," I said. "I'm really thankful when the sun's out and keeps us warm. Because I don't like it when it's gray and gloomy and cold. And it makes stuff grow and makes all the snow melt."

I noticed that once I gave thanks for these things, I started thinking differently about them; they became special gifts instead of ordinary things I usually just ignored and took for granted. And after a week of doing the Gratitude Jar with Lucas, I realized that I was starting to notice things around me a lot more.

Typically, I rushed to get somewhere or get something done. But now that I had to come up with gratitude each night, I went through my day in a completely different way. There was a little boy waiting expectantly for me to come up with something *really good* to be thankful for each night, so I had to start paying attention. And pay attention I did.

From the moment I woke up until the time I sat in Lucas's bed each night, I was on the lookout for things to be thankful for, and it completely changed my perspective. Looking for good things all day was a lot different from concentrating on the stuff that annoyed me, which is what I used to do. No wonder I used to be so crabby—all I ever saw was the bad. I never stopped to notice any of the good, much less give thanks for it.

This new way of thinking, of noticing good things and being grateful for them, was causing me to *feel* different too. It was subtle, like turning up the volume a notch, but it was there.

I felt happier.

I realized I'd never felt this good before, at least not to the point where I actually noticed. I felt a bit lighter, like there was a new bounce in my step; I was starting to see the world in color instead of black and white. The colors weren't super vivid yet, but they were forming around the edges.

Like I said, it was very subtle, but strong enough for me to notice something was shifting inside me.

And then others started to notice, too.

᭑ Almost two weeks after I'd started the Gratitude Jar, I met my friend Melanie for our monthly Moms' Night Out. She drank wine; I ate one of those chocolate molten lava cakes. I didn't miss alcohol at all anymore;

in fact, I found lava cake to be much more enjoyable than the usual bottle of booze I sucked down when we got together.

We chatted awhile about our kids, careers (Melanie is also a school counselor), relationships, and lives in general. About an hour in, Melanie quit talking midsentence about the business she and her twin sister were starting together and tilted her head. "You're different, Josie. What's going on with you?"

I shrugged. "What? Nothing. It's probably because I'm not drunk out of my mind right now." Usually by nine p.m. of Moms' Night Out, this mom was loaded.

"No, it's not that. I've been with you when you haven't been drinking before. You seem so . . ." She trailed off a few seconds and then shook her head. "I don't know, something." She took a sip of wine.

I dipped my spoon into chocolate lava and took a bite. "Well, I think it's the sober thing. Drunk Josie is totally different than sober Josie."

"No. It's not that." Melanie sighed. We sat in silence a few minutes while she mulled it over. Finally, she nodded. "I know what it is. You seem really happy. No, not just happy. You seem *joyous*," she said, putting emphasis on the word.

"What? Joyous? Seriously, Mel." I waved my spoon, dismissing her. "Joyous" had never been a word used to describe me before. I mean, I was feeling a little better these days, but joyous? That seemed like a stretch.

"That's so it," Melanie exclaimed. "I've been sitting here this entire time thinking something's changed with you since the last time I saw you. You seem so happy and, like, content. Yes, content! That's it. That's what I see when I look at you." She relaxed back into the booth.

I thought for a minute about what Melanie had said. I was definitely feeling happier, but being content wasn't something I'd noticed along with it. Probably because feeling content was something I'd never experienced before.

My husband gave me grief about this quality all the time. "Quit looking, Josie. You're always *looking* for something. Stop. Just be content where you're at." I had perpetual "the grass is greener somewhere else" syndrome. I could never follow his advice because I just couldn't help myself; I was never satisfied in the present moment. I wanted to be somewhere else, doing something else. Always.

But now, I realized Melanie was right. I *was* more content.

I realized my gratitude practice had caused this to happen without me even knowing it. Being more aware of the gifts I already had around me made me realize I didn't have to look for anything anymore. I already had what I needed, and I was okay. Content.

I had finally followed my husband's sage advice. I just hadn't realized it until Melanie pointed it out to me. I was really thankful to her right then for noticing. "Thanks, Mel," I said sincerely. I made a mental note to give gratitude for this conversation later.

"You're welcome." She shifted in her seat. "I need to tell you something else. You totally have a glow around you."

"What? A glow?" I started, but she cut me off.

"Yes! Listen to me. You have this light around you. Seriously." She asked again while taking another sip of wine, "So what are you doing? You've got to be doing something."

"Well, there is this little thing I've been doing each night with Lucas . . ." I launched into the story about my sessions with Maleah, learning about the Gratitude Jar, and practicing it with Lucas over the past few weeks. I told her I thought it might be the reason for my new-found happiness. And glowiness, too.

When I finished telling her everything, Melanie grabbed my hand across the table and stated, "You should keep doing that Gratitude Jar thing, because I've never seen you so happy the entire time I've known you. Gratitude certainly seems to agree with you, Josie."

GRATITUDE JAR DAY 11

"I'm gonna go first," said Lucas. "I'm thankful for, uh, um, my blankie because it keeps me very warm."

"That's good," I told him. "You've said that one before and that's okay. If you want to say ones you've said before, I'm okay with that," I explained to him.

Lucas shook his head. "I haven't said my blankie before, [he had], but I said my house before," he said impatiently.

I went along. "Okay. That's fine then, Lucas."

He went on, "I like to chew on my blankie. I like to put things on top of it. It's very big. It can even cover my pillow. It doesn't even fit on school cots."

"Whoa." I opened my eyes wide in exaggerated surprise.

"My blankie would just take up the whole cot and go over my head if you spread it all out. That's what it would do. Because it's very big," he said proudly.

"Cool. Do you know what I'm thankful for? I'm thankful for my body. Why do you think I'm thankful for my body?" I asked him.

Lucas sighed; he wasn't into the teachable moment I was trying to have with him. "I'm going to fall asleep," he said in a bored voice.

I ignored him and continued, "Our body does everything. We can eat, we can sleep, we can play. We can kiss, we can hug—"

Lucas interrupted and made a face. "Yuck! Kissing."

I laughed and went on, "But we can do all kinds of stuff. We can see, we can hear music—"

Lucas interrupted again, "But can they chew on blankies?"

"They can do everything."

"Even chew on blankies?" he asked again.

"Even chew on blankies," I answered.

☞ A few days later, Shawn and I lined up his parents to watch the boys so we could have a long overdue date night. My usual "hairball" (as Lucas called it when I pulled my hair into a messy bun) was now gone and styled. I had on some makeup and a girly dress instead of my typical mom gear of jeans and T-shirt. Lucas told me I looked "real fancy" that night during our Gratitude Jar time.

After I tucked in the boys and said good-bye to the in-laws, I walked outside to the car to meet Shawn. He was leaning against the driver's side, but when he saw me, he did a double take and walked over with an expression I hadn't seen since we first started dating. I mean, I knew I looked nice that evening, but I hadn't seen him look at me like that in years.

He grabbed my hand. "Hey. You look beautiful tonight. I mean, you always look beautiful, but tonight it seems even more so. You're glowing." I hadn't told

Shawn about my previous conversation with Melanie, so apparently my glowiness wasn't just an isolated incident.

"Thanks. This is what happens when I take a shower and actually do something with myself," I joked. We started toward the car together, holding hands.

Shawn continued, "Well, you look wonderful, and I'm really excited to go out with you tonight." He opened the passenger door for me. "I also think it's wonderful that you're doing the Gratitude Jar with Lucas. It's awesome he gets to share time with his mom reflecting on the good stuff of each day." He leaned over and kissed my forehead. "It's special. He's going to remember it the rest of his life." I got into the car and buckled my seat belt.

"I hope so. It's special time for me, too."

Before he turned on the ignition, he said, "One more thing. I'm glad you're back."

"What do you mean?" I asked.

"Old Josie is back," he explained, "the woman I married. You're finally out of that black hole you've been in forever." He started the car. "And you seem happier than I ever remember you being before. You're lighter." He took a serious tone. "I'm glad you found your way back. I missed you."

I smiled at him. "I missed me too." I leaned over and kissed him on the cheek. "It feels really good to be back."

⌐◦ Both Shawn and Melanie had made me notice that I was feeling a lot better. Being joyous, content— these were all things I'd never experienced before but now was starting to feel on an almost daily basis. I found it hard to believe a simple little jar could be responsible for these powerful new feelings, but it certainly seemed that way.

It was the only thing I'd been doing differently in the past couple weeks that could explain it. Granted, I'd made many changes over the course of the last few months, but none had caused me to experience these random bursts of pure joy.

And then, something fortuitous happened that convinced me the Gratitude Jar was absolutely the thing responsible for my new feelings.

⌐◦ Shortly after our date night, I was driving home with Lucas and Davis from the YMCA. As I pulled onto the parkway about a mile from our house, I noticed the car ahead of me was crawling along at only about ten miles per hour. Since there was no place for me to pass, I was forced to decelerate and trail behind them the rest of the way home.

Normally, since I'm a bit of a road rager, I would start directing angry, sarcastic comments toward them about how slow they were going. *Ten miles per hour in a thirty-five-mile-per-hour speed zone? I mean, come on, buddy. Let's go!*

But that day I had a completely different response to the situation. So much so that it kind of freaked me out because it was really out of character.

Instead of the usual road rage, I instead felt kind, loving, grateful feelings toward the person in the car in front of me. *Thank you for going slow today, random stranger,* I thought. *It's okay. I don't need to rush. It's a beautiful, sunny day.* My heart was literally full of joy for this person.

That has never, ever happened to me while driving before. My heart is usually filled with complete irritation instead.

As I was driving and feeling the love, I felt a huge thump at the bottom of my car. When I searched the street to see what caused it, I noticed the entire road was covered with giant potholes and I'd just run over one. That's when I realized why the car in front of me was going so slow—to avoid messing up their car driving over gigantic potholes.

I had a full-on gratitude explosion.

Thank you, car ahead of me! I would've just pulled onto the street, ignored the potholes, sped over them, and wrecked my car in the process. But you, oh you, wonderful person—you saved the day! And my car! I love you and am so thankful for your slowness!

I smiled to the person ahead, who would probably think I was crazy if they knew how I was feeling about them at the moment. But I didn't care; I was so full of love at the kindness of strangers, and the kindness of the world. I almost couldn't believe it was happening since it was so out of character for me, but I just couldn't help myself. I was completely overtaken by gratitude right there in my car.

That's when it really hit me that the gratitude practice Lucas and I had been doing was making a greater impact on me than I ever dreamed possible. My default mental state, which was negative, anxious, and irritated, was being replaced with a new state of mind. One that was loving, kind, and grateful.

Like Maleah said, *How you do one thing is how you do everything.* Once I started practicing gratitude, even though it was only a tiny bit, it started seeping across the rest of my life. I had moved from simply practicing it to living it. And I was becoming joyously happy in the process.

This was the first moment of many that made me realize gratitude was rewiring my brain and my heart.

ᦂ Speaking of the heart, Lucas had chosen to be thankful of his the next night. "I'm thankful for my heart because it keeps us alive with its blood that pumps around the body," he said while peering up at me from under his blanket.

"That's a good one, Lucas!" I was impressed; that was much better than my own gratitude, which had been the television. I was drawing a blank that night, but had watched a really great show earlier in the day that reminded me how mindless entertainment can be a fun distraction sometimes.

He continued in earnest, "And it has love in it. And everything is good in my heart." If we were in a gratitude competition that night, Lucas had just won by a landslide.

I thought about the sweetness and profoundness of his words, noticing my own heart for seemingly the first time. Right then it was full of love for this wise little boy lying beside me. I kissed his forehead and whispered, "You're right, Lucas. Thank you for that." Not only was I bursting with gratitude and joy now, but I was also learning important lessons from a four-year-old.

GRATITUDE JAR DAY 15

Sometimes our gratitude practice was just funny business.

"What are you thankful for tonight, Lucas?"

"I think of this when Mommy was trying to get to the tape recorder. Clothes. I'm thankful for clothes. It keeps our body warm and," Lucas lowered his voice, "you can't see your privates."

I laughed. "You're right about that."

"So what are you thankful for, Mommy?"

"You know how we're going to Asher's birthday tomorrow? I'm really thankful for birthday parties because they're super fun and we get to hang out with our friends and family."

Lucas looked up at me with a serious expression on his face. "Well, you know the bad thing about birthday parties—"

He stopped talking and looked around his room as if he was paranoid someone else was listening. He started again, "You know the bad thing about birthday parties, Mommy? Can I tell you about it?" He motioned for me to come closer. He was acting as if he was about to betray a big secret amongst four-year-olds.

I leaned in. "Sure. Tell me."

He cupped his hand over my ear and whispered, "Sometimes too much sugar gets in them."

I started laughing. "That's true, Lucas. Definitely true."

༭ It didn't occur to me Lucas was experiencing just as many benefits from our nightly thank yous as I was until one day when we were out driving again. This incident happened about two and a half weeks after we started the Gratitude Jar (for whatever reason, my major revelations, both gratitude-related and not, seem to occur while I'm in the car. Is that a thing? It's possible I could be spending too much time driving.)

On our way to the store, Lucas was really quiet in the backseat. Usually he was chatting away, asking about road signs or giving me a play-by-play of what his baby brother was doing in his car seat. But today, he was silent. He obviously had things on his mind so I let him be. Frankly, it was nice to have some quiet time for myself.

About halfway to our destination, Lucas came out of his silence and asked, "Do you know what, Mommy?"

I glanced at him in the rearview mirror. "What, sweetie?" He was staring out the window thoughtfully.

He turned to look at me in the mirror reflection and said quietly, "I really appreciate my life. I really, really, really do."

I stopped, taken off guard by what he had just said. "Really? That's great, sweetie!" I felt a lump start to form in my throat.

Lucas stared back out the window and started nodding like he'd just made up his mind about something. "Yeah, I really like it a lot. My life. I appreciate everything."

I felt the mom tears coming on. "Thank you for saying that, Lucas. I'm really glad you feel that way." I took a deep breath and said to him. "I feel that way about my life now, too." And I meant it.

That's when I realized Lucas's head and heart were being rewired by gratitude as well.

GRATITUDE JAR DAY 19

"What are you thankful for tonight?"

Lucas pulled up his blanket and yawned, "I'm thankful for, ah, um, sleep. Because it make you really strong and it's good for your brain and stuff." He yawned again. "It's everything."

He turned to me and asked, "What are you thankful for, Mommy?"

I thought about my own gratitude for a minute. "Well, I went out to lunch with my friend Jess today, and I'm really thankful for friends. Because friends, they're fun, right?" Lucas nodded. I continued, "It's fun to play with friends—"

Lucas interrupted, "Yeah! I play with Caden. He's a friend."

"Yes. He's a friend," I agreed.

He continued, "Baby Davis, he's a brother so I play with him too. He's like a friend for life."

I smiled, "Yes, he is."

꒥ Our nightly gratitude had become such a special bonding experience for Lucas and me; I felt bad his little brother Davis couldn't do it with us. Davis was only nine months old and a long way away from being able

43

to participate, but he came up pretty regularly in our nightly gratitudes, so it was kind of like he was there with us.

"I'm thankful for my baby brother because he brang a lot of love in our house," Lucas said. "And he's very, very cutie, even. He's the cutest thing in the world. I kiss him and touch him because he's so soft. And babies are so funny."

Lucas stopped and grabbed my hand. "They're like—" He started fake chewing on my hand like his baby brother did. Davis was in the phase where everything was a chew toy, especially hands and fingers. Lucas dropped my hand and continued, "And babies are like AAAGGHHHH!" Lucas screamed at the top of his lungs and fell onto his bed, waving his arms and legs around.

He stopped screaming and gave me a knowing look. "They scream a lot."

I laughed. "They sure do."

Lucas asked several times when Davis could do the Gratitude Jar with us. I knew it would be a long time before that happened, so I decided to get creative and find another way for him to join us. So one night, I switched our gratitude routine and brought the jar to the dinner table. Besides including Davis, I thought it would be nice to include Shawn as well.

When we were all seated, I pointed to the Star Wars Easter basket in the center of the table. "We're going to each talk about what we're thankful for. It could be something that happened today or just something in general that you're thankful for. So, whoever wants to go first—"

Shawn chimed in, "Lucas, why don't you go first?"

"I'm thankful for my mom," he said while chewing his spaghetti.

"Aw, thanks, sweetie," I said and reached over to tousle his hair.

Lucas turned to his baby brother. "What are you thankful for, baby Davis?"

Davis reached across the table and grabbed the digital recorder out of my hand, put it in his mouth, and started chewing on it. Laughter broke out across the table. I pried the recorder out of Davis's hands and put it out of reach. "I think he's thankful for food," Shawn said jokingly.

"Can I go?" Shawn asked. I nodded. "I'm thankful for this wonderful family day we had together. Yeah?" He looked around at everyone for agreement. Shawn had the day off from work and we had all gone to the zoo together.

Baby Davis started flapping his arms around and squealing; he was excited, trying to tell us something. Lucas peered closely at him. "I think he said he's thankful for his mom," he concluded.

Shawn grabbed my hand under the table and smiled. "I think he said he's thankful for his mom, too."

I beamed. I looked around the table at these wonderful people surrounding me, and I couldn't believe just a few short months ago I had thought they would have been better off without me. Did I really use to feel that way? It didn't seem possible, almost like it was someone else who'd been thinking those dark things. It certainly wasn't joyful, content, blissed-out me.

I was so thankful I'd brought the Gratitude Jar to dinner with me that evening. It made me realize how far I'd come and how much I truly loved being with my family. A few months ago, I'd wished for them to replace me with a newer mom who would love them better. I realized now that wish had been granted. Only it wasn't a different person I'd been replaced with; it was a different me. A much better version.

My original purpose for using the Gratitude Jar was to improve my relationship with Lucas and feel more connected to him. After only a few short weeks of gratitude together, I was happy to report that mission was totally and completely accomplished. This little activity had brought us, and the rest of my family, closer together than I ever thought possible.

CHAPTER FIVE

MIRACLES

"*Eucharisteo—thanksgiving—always precedes the miracle.*"

—ANN VOSKAMP, *ONE THOUSAND GIFTS:*
A DARE TO LIVE FULLY RIGHT WHERE YOU ARE

Yes, things were definitely looking up. Emotionally, I felt better than ever. My relationships with everyone had improved, and I felt like I was finally living with purpose. Gratitude had certainly done a lot for me, but there was still an area of my life that needed fixing:

Money.

We were broke out of our minds.

No amount of gratitude seemed to make the money we desperately needed magically appear. Even though I was feeling great these days, there was still a perpetual knot in my stomach about how we were going to make it financially each month. We'd cut out every possible luxury like cable and restaurants and bought our clothes secondhand. I made *everything* from scratch: food, cleaning products, etc. Everyone was forced to wear sweaters or use blankets to save on the energy bill no matter how freezing it was (which is probably why Lucas mentioned being cold several times during our gratitude sessions together).

I watched every single dollar like a hawk, but every month we were still short. I'd lost count of how many times we'd overdrafted our bank account, and every credit card we owned was maxed out. I'd tried applying for several jobs to supplement our income but never received a single call back. We were in the thick of the recession, and jobs just weren't available.

At that point, like so many others in our country at the time, Shawn and I contemplated walking away from our home. But it didn't make financial sense since our mortgage payment was lower than the insanely expensive rents in the Twin Cities, so we stayed put and tried to figure out a way to make it work.

But it wasn't working. And I didn't know what else I could cut out to make it much longer. I went over our grocery budget for what felt like the hundredth time to figure out how to make it stretch even further, and I added meat and cheese to the list of luxuries that also needed to go. I scoured cookbooks for recipes to make pasta and potatoes more interesting with as few ingredients as possible.

Thankfully, my boys never complained about the food I served even though it was usually bland and there weren't second helpings available. All of us had a silent understanding that this was just how it was, and we had to make do the best we could.

But I was over it. I wanted more money.

❧ To get more money, I needed more hours at my job. Over the years, my part-time position as a school counselor had been cut to the point where I now only worked a few hours a week. I had gone from full-time to part-time several years ago when I first had Lucas because my mother-in-law offered to do daycare for free a couple days a week. When we ran the numbers of me working full-time and paying full-time daycare versus me working part-time with free part-time daycare, part-time won out (daycare is crazy expensive in Minnesota). Plus, it would be nice to be home.

But as our school district budget was cut, so were my hours—and now I was barely working. My boss told me at the beginning of the school year that my slender new schedule was temporary, and I would get more hours the next school year. I was hoping that was the case because the money we had in savings to cover the year of me not working was completely gone.

While Lucas and I were in the middle of our thirty days of gratitude, my boss called me into his office and told me he needed to talk with me about my position for next year. I was sure he was going to tell me I was finally going to get more hours, because this gratitude thing was making me feel invincible. Only good things were going to come my way from now on.

Unfortunately, it didn't happen that way.

Instead, my boss told me there was no way I would get more hours, maybe ever, with where our school budget was headed. I was devastated. I had been counting on getting more hours, not less. I left his office, holding back tears until I got back to my own where I could shut the door and cry. What the heck was I going to do? I started to put my resume together to look for a new part-time job, because there was no way I could afford another year like this last one we'd had.

I was disappointed, but as the day went on I started to feel okay about leaving since I had a lot of complaints about my job anyway. Besides low pay and skimpy hours, there were other things I didn't like: having to travel around the district and work in four different schools, a coworker whose favorite pastime was gossiping about me, doing work I wasn't creatively fulfilled by, and a whole host of others.

But I was terrified of finding a new job. We were living in one of the worst economic periods on record and there was a strong possibility I wouldn't find *anything*. And then what? I could continue in my current job, only working a couple hours a week, but we just couldn't survive on that income much longer. We were at the end of our rope financially. I needed more money. Now.

That night, sitting in bed with Lucas, I didn't feel thankful for anything. My mind had been running over worst-case scenarios all day, and I was on the verge of an epic panic attack. Even though my anxiety had been under control for a while, this situation was causing it to flare up again.

I stared at the Gratitude Jar sitting on Lucas's bed with him tucked in next to it and decided to flip the switch. I knew if I kept worrying about job and money stuff, my anxiety was going to take control of me. I didn't want that to happen again.

So I decided, starting right then and there, to quit all the bitching, complaining, and focusing on the negatives about my job and money—and start giving gratitude for them instead.

I figured this gratitude stuff seemed to be helping me in other parts of my life; maybe it would with this too. It couldn't hurt anyway. Besides, I didn't really know what else to do and it was the only thing I could think of to avoid having a massive anxiety attack right there in Lucas's bed. So I took a deep breath and asked him, "Do you want me to go first, or do you go first tonight?"

"I want to go first."

"Okay. What are you thankful for, Lucas?"

He started pointing at things around his room. "My toys and my books and my blanket and my stuffed animals and my posters. All the stuff I like to play with and read and the things that make me comfy. I enjoy them."

"That's really nice. Do you know what I'm thankful for?"

"What?" He pulled up his blanket and turned toward me.

I took a breath, trying really hard to mean what I was about to say even though the exact opposite was going through my brain. "I'm thankful both your daddy and I have jobs. It gives us money so we can have our house and food and clothes." I realized it felt weird to say because I was usually negative about it.

I paused a second to think of more, thinking if I did, maybe I would get cosmic extra credit and money would just fall out of the sky or something. It was magical thinking, but whatever, I was desperate. I continued, "I'm also thankful your dad and I work in jobs we both like doing and get to help people. Your daddy is a teacher and I'm a counselor, and we both have jobs where we get to help kids feel better and solve their problems. It's really rewarding." I let out a breath and relaxed back onto Lucas's pillow.

Lucas said knowingly, "I get to help people too, because I'm a nice kid. Being a nice kid is kind of like helping people."

I smiled. Blame it on Lucas to make a great point that brought me back to what was *really* important. "You're right, Lucas. Being a nice kid is totally like helping people." I tucked him in and said goodnight, praying everything would work out. Because if it didn't, we were in huge trouble.

༄ I made good on my promise to continue my gratitude practice outside of my nightly jar time with Lucas. Throughout the day, whenever I noticed a negative thought about money or my job come up, I immediately turned it around with gratitude:

I wish I worked more. I need more hours. Being home all the time drives me crazy. *I'm thankful I get to stay home and be with my children all day. I'm lucky since most of the moms I know work full-time and don't get to see their kids as much as I do.*

How are we going to afford anything? We have no money. *I'm thankful we've been able to survive on one income for as long as we have. I'm also thankful for the skills I've learned from being so frugal: cooking from scratch, gardening my own herbs and vegetables, managing money better, doing my own home repairs.*

I can't stand so-and-so that I work with. All she ever does is talk crap about me to everyone. *I'm thankful I work with someone who notices my flaws and forces me to confront them. It makes me better at my job. Plus, most of the people I work with genuinely like me and have positive relationships with me. Thank you.*

From doing this all day, every day, I realized I was

in a constant negative thought loop about my job and money. It seemed like every five minutes I was thinking a worrisome, pessimistic thought about these two things; it was no wonder I was having problems with them. They had become self-fulfilling prophecies: I didn't like my job, so the Universe found a way for me to lose it. Same with money.

GRATITUDE JAR DAY 22

"I've got to think about what I'm thankful for tonight, honey."

Lucas nodded. "Me too."

"I'm trying to think of something I haven't done yet." I paused, contemplating.

"Me too," Lucas repeated. "We've done a lot of them."

"We've done a lot of stuff, that's for sure." We sat in silence for a moment while we thought of our "thankful things," as Lucas was now calling them. *Can we do our thankful things tonight, Mommy?* Lucas would ask at dinner. It was cute.

"Oh, I got one," I said. "I'm thankful all of us are healthy right now. None of us has any sickness, like, we're not barfing or have colds or the flu or anything like that. I'm glad we're healthy."

Lucas was hurt. "You go first."

"Um, yeah I did." I realized he always went first—it was his thing. I hoped he wouldn't be too upset about it.

"I wanna go first," he cried. Too late.

"Okay, you go then," I said soothingly to reassure him.

Lucas calmed down. "So let's switch this over. Now you're gonna be thankful for a different thing after me," he instructed.

"Okay, well, you better go then."

Lucas wiggled around as he tried to come up with something. "Um, err." I could tell he was having a tough time. Finally, he said, "Ah, um, doors."

"Doors? Why are you thankful for doors?" I asked.

"Because you can get to places with them," he explained.

"How do you get to places?"

Lucas pointed at his door. "There's some in your house. If you want to get to my room, you just turn the door and go into it. That's what it's like." He nodded. "And when you drive to something and open the door, then you're in the place."

I smiled. "That's good. I never thought to be thankful for doors."

"And what are you thankful for, mommy?" he asked.

I gave him a pointed look. "I'm thankful everybody's super healthy right now."

Lucas rolled his eyes. "Okay, Mommy."

"I thought that was a good one."

⮂ After a few weeks of actively turning my negative work-related thoughts around with gratitude, I noticed my stress levels dropped dramatically. I also noticed I felt more optimistic and actually enjoyed being there. That was a first.

And then one day, while sitting in a meeting with my counseling department, I started feeling downright joyous to be there. The feeling came out of nowhere; it was very similar to the gratitude explosion I had while driving over those giant potholes, but I was filled with this overwhelming love and appreciation for the people sitting at the table around me. I realized I loved my job.

Like, totally and completely adored it. It was as if gratitude had hijacked my brain to where all I could see were the positives about my work situation:

I had it really good only working one day a week and being able to afford to stay home with the kids.

I liked the people I worked with, even the one whose mission it was to get me fired.

I really enjoyed the work I did; it was interesting, creative, and emotionally fulfilling.

I didn't mind traveling to four different schools; it was nice to have the flexibility and meet new people.

I completely forgot what I ever complained about in the first place! I couldn't believe I had spent so many years thinking negatively about it. Gratitude had completely shifted my thoughts on it, and now I didn't want to leave.

As for the money stuff, well, okay, I was still stressed. I hadn't found a new job or won any of the sweepstakes I entered daily, so I had to work extra hard to replace my pessimistic money thoughts with gratitude. But I was like the little engine that could and trudged along: we have a house, we have food, we have clothes, thank you, thank you, chug, chug, chug.

I wouldn't say I loved my money situation from practicing gratitude on it, but at least I wasn't having an anxiety attack about it, so that was an improvement.

And then some crazy, miraculous stuff started happening.

↶ Shortly after I started feeling the love for my job, I coincidentally ran into the woman who was in charge of the Advanced Placement (AP) program at our school. I asked her how it was going, since AP was a huge amount of work. She freely admitted wishing she could pass the AP program off to someone else. She was an almost-retired teacher who wanted to make it official.

She had heard I was looking for more hours and asked if I wanted to take the AP program from her. Did I? Yes, please! I gave a silent prayer at my good luck of running into her that day and practically ran to my boss's office to discuss it with him. When I got there, I asked if I could come in to talk with him about my position for next year. He gave me a strange look and motioned for me to sit down.

I asked what the look was about. He said, "Well, it's just a coincidence you came in today, Josie, because I was just about to call you in myself about your position."

Oh. No. I braced myself; my excitement at the possibility of taking over AP was quickly deflated at the thought I was going to hear more bad news about my position. *Please, no more cuts.* I waited to ask him about AP until I heard what he had to say first. I held my breath and waited.

He started, "The budget wasn't as bad as we originally thought and we'd like to add more hours to your position for the upcoming school year. We think what you're doing is really important and want to expand on it."

I let out my breath and stared at him. *What? I'm getting more hours? Expand?* I wasn't expecting that. I sat there and stared at him a moment. "Um, that's great!" I finally got out.

I thanked him profusely, then told him about the conversation I'd just had in the hallway about taking over the AP program. *Would this be a good way to expand the position?* I asked.

He thought for a minute, and then gave a definite "yes." He said it was a great idea and would add even more hours to my position.

Then as an afterthought he mentioned, "I think you'd be more effective if you only worked at one school, instead of traveling to four. What do you think about staying at South Campus and focusing your efforts there instead of traveling and spreading yourself thin? An empty office just opened in the South Campus Career Center that you could use."

"Err, really?" I stared at him again. I couldn't believe this was happening; South Campus was the school I dreamed about working in exclusively. The staff was incredible and the students were at the age level I enjoyed working with the most. This was the exact job scenario I'd been wanting for years, and it was now being handed to me on a silver platter.

"Yes! That sounds great," I agreed and nodded so vigorously I felt my neck cramp. "Thank you so much, Tim!"

He said he would call Human Resources and let them know about the change and congratulated me on a job well done. I shook his hand and thanked him again, left his office, and had a full-on gratitude explosion in the hallway.

Crisis averted! I have a job! And not just any job, my ideal job! Thank you, thank you, thank you!

I felt tears of gratitude well in my eyes. Teachers walked by and stared at the weird half-dance, half-cry I was doing in the hallway, but I didn't care. I was so relieved and thankful to have a job with enough hours to feed my family. When I got back to my office I cried again, but this time it was tears of joy.

We had a celebration in our house that night, a nice dinner with meat and cheese I'd bought special after work that day. I even turned up the thermostat a bit.

GRATITUDE JAR DAY 25

"Tell us what you're thankful for, Mino," Lucas said as he pet our cat Kamino. She was lying between us on his bed that night. She meowed at him in response.

I scratched her ears. "I think she's thankful for your blanket."

"You know what she said?" Kamino started to purr loudly, loving the attention.

"What?" I asked.

"Meow. I think that's how she tells us her thankful fors," Lucas explained.

"So what do you think she said, Lucas?"

Lucas thought about it a minute. "Her cat food." He laid down next to Kamino and spoke softly to her, "Thankful for your cat food, Mino?" She purred in response. "I'm thankful for, uh, this beautiful weekend. This beautiful weekend we had."

"What about it was your favorite? What about it was beautiful?" I asked.

"Oh, just the snow that's melting and you can see the

grass more. 'Cause it's turning to spring." Lucas turned to face me. "What are you thankful for, Mommy?"

"I'm thankful for my mom and dad, your Grandma Karen and Grandpa Chuck, because they took really good care of me when I was growing up. I love them very much. They're really good, nice people. Good, nice parents."

"But what did they look like when they were young?" Lucas asked.

I laughed; my parents weren't *that* old. But to a four-year-old, anybody over the age of ten was probably ancient. "We'll have to ask to see some pictures next time we see them," I said, still smiling.

Lucas rolled over and pulled up his blanket, satisfied with my answer. "Okay. Good night, Mommy."

☙ I decided to continue practicing gratitude about my job because of what had happened. Honestly, I didn't want to jinx it. I still couldn't believe I would be working in my *dream* job for the upcoming school year.

Shortly after my conversation in Tim's office, I got an email from Human Resources with the subject: "Contract Change." I felt my stomach drop; maybe it was too good to be true. Human Resources was going to tell me there had been a mistake; I wouldn't get more hours because of the budget or some other reason. I stared at the email a long time, and prepared for the worst before opening it.

Thankfully, that wasn't the case at all.

What the email really said was all the part-time employees in my school district just had their contracts adjusted, and they were getting a raise. Which meant, I was getting a raise. Congratulations!

I almost fell out of my chair when I read it.

As you can imagine, gratitude explosion part two happened.

A raise? Yes! Woo-hoo! Thank you! Thank you!

I felt a huge wave of relief. My job was getting more hours, and I was getting more money. We were going to make it. We could eat, with second helpings even. Maybe we could even *go out* to eat once in a while. I couldn't remember the last time I'd been to a restaurant. Years, probably. I sighed, thanking God again for what felt like the zillionth time since I began my gratitude practice.

And just when I thought things couldn't get any better, one of my coworkers informed me that the gossipy coworker who'd made my life miserable for so many years was transferring to another high school. To the high school I *wasn't* going to be working at. I wouldn't see her again—for a very long time. That was the cherry on top of this series of extraordinary events.

It was like I had just dialed up the Universe, asked for exactly what I wanted—and it magically appeared.

I couldn't believe it; things were falling into place effortlessly. It was miraculous because my job and money had been such a struggle for me for so many years. And now, everything was working out beautifully. Easily. Effortlessly.

Why didn't I figure this out before? If I knew all this amazing stuff was going to happen from simply giving gratitude instead of complaining, I would have quit all my bitching a long time ago. It would have saved me years of heartache and worrying how we were going to live day-to-day.

I was never going to think a negative thought about my job or money, again. Period.

❧ I learned a life-changing lesson from that experience: thinking about and giving thanks for what you want produces more of it, while thinking and complaining about what you don't want produces more of it. It's what new age gurus and spiritual leaders have been saying for centuries, but I didn't actually believe it—until now.

I could physically *see* the results of my gratitude practice in my daily life now. My new gratitude-focused thoughts were creating a different reality than the one I used to live in, the one where I only saw the negative side of things. Now, I was living in a completely new world, and it was much better than the one I lived in before.

I have a strong suspicion if I'd continued my cycle of complaining about my career and lack of money, I'd probably still be out looking for a job.

◠ "I'm thankful for my school. I'm thankful for my school 'cause it helps us learn. My school does. And I do fun projects and play there. And I listen to the teachers," Lucas said proudly.

"That's good, that's really important."

Lucas continued, "And be quiet at nap time."

I smiled. "That's good too."

"And it's really fun being at school," Lucas went on, "but when I get older and turn into a grown-up, I don't have to have school. I get to have work."

I was curious if my past negativity about work had rubbed off on him. I hoped not. "What do you think about work some day?"

"Gonna be pretty fun." Lucas sighed. "But there's going to be lots of annoying teenager kids."

I laughed; Lucas had definitely heard me complain. But to be fair, it probably wasn't just me he overheard; Shawn taught high school English at an alternative high school and had his own share of bad days. No matter how much gratitude I gave for teenagers, they were still teenagers at the end of the day. But I loved working with them despite their challenges—especially now after my newfound appreciation for my job.

"Do you know why teenagers are annoying?" Lucas asked.

"No. Tell me. Why?"

He nodded seriously. "They're like toddlers. Crabby toddlers."

I laughed aloud. "Crabby toddlers! Oh, Lucas." I leaned over and kissed the top of his head. "You crack me up, kid." I guess he had heard some of my complaining, but let's be fair—he nailed it. Teenagers and toddlers were remarkably similar in many ways, especially in the midst of a temper tantrum.

Looking at Lucas lying there with our Gratitude Jar between us, my heart was full. I felt so grateful for my job, my life, and this wonderful little boy sitting next to me who always brightened my spirit.

I was a long way from the person who used to stare at the bedroom ceiling, feeling empty. "I love you. Thanks for always making me smile." I kissed his cheek and put the Gratitude Jar on his nightstand. "Good night." Yes, things were definitely going to be okay.

CHAPTER SIX

FREEDOM

"To be grateful is to recognize the Love of God in everything He has given us—and He has given us everything. Every breath we draw is a gift of His love, every moment of existence is a grace, for it brings with it immense graces from Him.

"Gratitude therefore takes nothing for granted, is never unresponsive, and is constantly awakening to new wonder and to praise of the goodness of God. For the grateful person knows that God is good, not by hearsay but by experience. And that is what makes all the difference."

—THOMAS MERTON

As we neared the end of our thirty days of gratitude, it was obvious Lucas had started to peter out. He was having a really tough time coming up with things to be thankful for each night, so it was a good thing we only had a few days left.

Really, I was just impressed he'd lasted for as long as he did. "What are you thankful for tonight, Lucas?" I asked while sorting through the slips of paper in our Gratitude Jar. There were a lot in there. He wiggled around on his bed. "I'm thinking about it."

"That's good, I am too. I think I know what I'm thankful for, but I'll wait until you go first."

"Okay, I'm thankful for this part of my bed," Lucas pointed at the wooden ball screwed to the corner post of his bed.

"You were already thankful for that." Lucas had been thankful for his headboard the night before. Like I said, he was really stretching to come up with his thankful things lately; for the past couple nights it had been an item of furniture from his room.

"No! Not my headboard! Thankful for the little ball things," he explained as he unscrewed the small wooden ball from his bed. He lifted his arm out and showed it to me.

"Can you try to come up with something better than that, sweetie?"

"Why?" He started passing the wooden ball from one hand to the other.

"Because I'd like you to try to come up with something else besides parts of your bed. You could also be thankful for things that happened to you today, too," I hinted. "Can you put the ball back on the bed, please?"

Lucas was getting clumsy with the ball and I could see clearly what was about to happen next.

CRASH! Lucas dropped the ball on the hardwood floor and it landed with a huge bang. I grabbed the ball and screwed it back onto the bed. I took a deep breath and started again, "Why don't you think of something you're thankful for that happened today, maybe?" I hinted again.

Lucas, obviously not listening, jumped out of bed and started doing somersaults on his blue shag rug. I felt the mom irritation kick in. "Can you sit in your bed, please? Can you sit down? *Now*."

Lucas heard the tone of my voice and quickly hopped back into bed. "Uh, ah, um, I'm thankful for the floor 'cause we don't fall. There's not, like, little pits you fall in. We have a floor." I sighed; at least it wasn't bedroom furniture again. And the pits thing *was* somewhat creative. "Okay, I'll take it."

"So what are you thankful for, Mommy?" he asked.

"Well, can you turn around and listen to me?" Lucas was staring up at the posters by his bed, not paying attention to me in the slightest. I sighed for what felt like the hundredth time; it was one of those nights.

He finally turned around and asked politely, "What are you thankful for, Mommy?"

"Much better. Do you know what I'm thankful for? I'm thankful for your daddy. Do you know why?" Lucas shook his head. "Because he's responsible for me knowing all the people I love the most in my life: G-Ma, Poppa, Uncle Zach, Aunt Emma. It's all because of Daddy. And without him, I wouldn't have you or baby Davis."

Lucas was silent awhile and then said softly, "That's very, very good, Mommy."

꩜ Even though Lucas was winding down on our nightly gratitude, I was sad that it was coming to an end. So much good had happened over the past month from doing the Gratitude Jar together, I was nervous if I stopped that everything would go back to how it used to be. And I would end up in my black hole again. I didn't want to go back there. Ever.

But with how I felt now, I knew that probably wouldn't happen.

I had transformed.

I felt joyous, content, alive. And others besides Shawn and Melanie noticed too; friends and relatives commented on how different I seemed, how happy I was. Even random strangers stopped me in the street to tell me I was glowing—then asked where it came from. I just smiled and told them my story about a little boy and a Gratitude Jar.

I kept thinking back to that moment I went on my knees and asked God for an intervention; so much had changed since then. I used to wake up in the morning with a knot in my stomach about the "crap" coming in the day ahead: my whiny kids, my annoying husband, my lack of money, my perpetual hangover. It seemed so unbelievable to me I used to feel that way.

Because when I woke up in the morning now, I automatically closed my eyes and pictured all the amazing things I had to look forward to: my loving husband and children, a beautiful home, working in my dream job, nourishing food for mealtimes, a healthy body, a beautiful planet to live on, supportive friends, a benevolent God who answered all my prayers, and on and on and on.

Then, after thinking of all these wonderful things, I opened my eyes and gave a huge, heartfelt, smiling *thank you* to all that is.

Honestly, I am completely and totally overwhelmed with gratitude for all things each and every morning I wake up. Like, my heart is bursting with joy and thankfulness. I realize that sounds corny, but it's 100 percent true. I asked God to bring me what served my highest and best purpose, and God answered through a psychic, a jar, and a four-year-old.

God really does work in mysterious ways. My prayer was answered beautifully.

GRATITUDE JAR DAY 27

"What are you thankful for tonight, Lucas?" Both of us were snuggled under his fleece blanket, keeping each other warm. It was one of those freezing-cold spring days. Spring was really just extended winter here in Minnesota, and I was still keeping the thermostat low. Old habits die hard.

"I'm thankful for breakfast and dinner and lunch." Lucas started rubbing his belly and making chomping noises. "And they taste so good when I eat all the food. Know one thing I really like?"

"What?"

He stopped chomping and said seriously, "Peanut butter and jelly sandwiches."

"I like those too."

"Me too," he continued, "and I eat string cheese with them and pretzels. Then I get a carrot and eat some apricots. But I drink milk with lunch and breakfast."

"You're making me hungry. Food is definitely a good thing to be thankful for." I thought about my own gratitude for the night. "You know what, Lucas? Tonight I'm thankful for Mother Earth because she gives us all the food you just talked about. And water, a beautiful place to live, really cool animals, air to breathe. Earth is pretty awesome."

"Earth is my favorite planet ever," Lucas said with a nod.

"Mine too."

He started again, "I'm thankful for Earth because it gives us water and food and it's very pretty. We live on the land. I like everything about the Earth. But it's a very expensive planet."

"It's an expensive planet?"

"Yes." He looked at me knowingly. "Because it breaks."

I smiled. "You're right. Earth does break sometimes, doesn't it?"

꩜ The other major shifts that happened in my awareness from practicing gratitude were two things I now began to notice constantly that I had never noticed before. One of those things was Earth. Frankly, I never used to give Earth the time of day.

I never stopped to notice the beauty that surrounded me. Immediately after I started the Gratitude Jar, like right after I dropped my first slip of paper into the jar, that changed. Earth became a constant source of inspiration for my nightly gratitude. All I had to do was walk outside and look around a minute, and I could find something to be thankful for. I couldn't believe I never saw Her before.

I noticed Earth so much that it affected my ability to arrive on time. For example, while I was out driving to a meeting across town one day a few weeks into gratitude, I had to pull my car over to stop and look at a lake.

Sounds crazy, I know, but true. That day the lake was clear as glass and the sun was reflecting on it in a beautiful way, so I stopped. I pulled my car into the parking lot by the beach, got out, and sat on a picnic table awhile and just stared.

My heart was filled with gratitude by how breathtaking the view was. It was just one of the many lakes we have here in Minnesota, and I'd seen hundreds of these same types of views before, but now, after practicing gratitude, I saw it differently.

I gave a simple thank you to the Earth, got back into my car, and drove to my meeting. I was a few minutes late, but nobody noticed. It was completely worth it.

That event never would have happened pre-gratitude, but now, something like that happens to me almost every day. Sometimes it's a tree, a thunderstorm, birds chirping, flowers blooming; there's always something in nature that forces me to stop and look and fills me with gratitude. Gratitude completely opened my eyes to Earth's beauty and never-ending generosity. I'm glad I can finally see Her so clearly now.

Gratitude also opened my eyes to something else I never saw around me. There's one other important thing I never gave much thought to before, but now noticed constantly. That I felt with me all the time.

God.

࿊ Every single time I gave gratitude, even for the littlest thing, I felt I touched a presence greater than myself. It's like gratitude opened the channel between me and God and I could touch God, if only for a minute. Every major religious book is filled with verses about expressing gratitude to God, and I believe that is because it's the best way to reach Him:

> Give thanks in all circumstances; for this is the will of God in Christ Jesus for you.
>
> —1 Thessalonians

> You have no cause for anything but gratitude and joy.
>
> —Buddha

> Be content with what you have; rejoice in the way things are. When you realize there is nothing lacking, the whole world belongs to you.
>
> —Lao Tzu

> Gratitude for the abundance you have received is the best insurance that abundance will continue.
>
> —Prophet Muhammad

This is the day the Lord has made; let us rejoice and be glad in it.

—PSALM 118:24

Gratitude gives us eyes to see God, Earth, beauty, love, joy, and abundance. Everything we never knew was already right there in front of us, waiting. We just needed gratitude to open our eyes.

And to appreciate the God who put it all there for us.

It's a lot different to say "thank you" to God instead of asking for stuff. That's the way I used to pray. Help me, God. Do this for me, God. I'm mad at you, God, fix it.

I don't pray like that anymore. The only prayer I say now is *Thank you.*

Similar to what happened to the rabbi in the parable at the beginning of this book, living in gratitude made me realize I loved God not for what God could do for me, but because God simply was. God didn't need to do anything anymore; I had been blessed beyond belief and I wanted to simply spend the rest of my life thanking God for everything I'd been blessed with.

So just like the rabbi who realized his love for God was motivated by pure love and not personal gain, I realized mine was as well.

I, too, was finally free of myself at last.

GRATITUDE JAR DAY 30

Our last day of doing the Gratitude Jar together, coincidentally, happened to fall on Easter Sunday (I mean, God has the best timing, right?).

Lucas and I sat in his bed together, his new Star Wars Easter basket next to the old one that was now our Gratitude Jar. Lucas looked through his new basket at all the candy and toys he'd gotten while I looked through our slips of gratitude in the basket from last year. It was filled to the top.

I felt nostalgic reading through them and thought about how our lives had transformed from the first night we started saying thank you. I couldn't believe how much had changed, and how different I felt. Joyous. Content. Spiritual. All because of a little jar.

"What are you thankful for today, Mommy?" Lucas asked. I stopped digging through our gratitudes and turned toward him. "I'm thankful for this awesome Easter Sunday we had."

"Me too," he agreed.

"It was so much fun," I said and gave him a squeeze around the shoulders.

Lucas nodded. "So we just have one."

I smiled. "Yes. We just have one."

CHAPTER SEVEN

HOW TO DO THE GRATITUDE JAR

"Thankfulness is the beginning of gratitude. Gratitude is the completion of thankfulness. Thankfulness may consist merely of words. Gratitude is shown in acts."

—HENRI FREDERIC AMIEL

You probably have a pretty good idea of how to do the Gratitude Jar from reading the book, but I know there might be a few of you who skipped directly to this chapter to get started right away. Either is fine, as long as you give the Gratitude Jar a try for the next thirty days. I guarantee if you do, it will change your life in extraordinary ways like it did my own.

Maleah's original suggestion was thirty days and I completely agree. It is the perfect amount of time to

experience all the major benefits that come from practicing gratitude. It's also enough time to turn it from a
practice to a permanent habit. And you are obviously free
to continue longer than thirty days if you wish or to stop
and come back to it again at a later time. I've since made
the Gratitude Jar a family tradition in our home. Each
year in the thirty days leading up to Christmas and Easter, we do the Gratitude Jar together as a family. It's been
a wonderful way to keep our gratitude goodness going.

Now, I know there are a few of you who might be
thinking, "Josie, I'm inspired by your story. I'm going to
start living with gratitude all the time the minute I put
this book down."

I totally get where you're coming from and admire
your enthusiasm, but unfortunately, it doesn't work that
way. We can't just *will* ourselves to change; we have to
practice a new habit every day in order to change the
ingrained thoughts that lead to our current behaviors.
But the good news is, you only have to practice a few
minutes of gratitude each day in order to change the
destructive thoughts getting in the way of living a life
full of abundance and joy. Because when it comes to
gratitude, a little goes a long way.

By just spending a few minutes in gratitude each day,
you'll notice your thoughts start to shift in a remarkably
short period of time. Most of us aren't used to practicing gratitude, so the effects are noticeable immediately

since you're using a part of your brain that probably hasn't been used much before, if at all.

As you notice your thoughts shifting, you'll also notice your mood shifting. You'll feel better. Joyous, even. And when you're in that joyous, happy place— that's when the miracles start happening.

I know, I know, it sounds too good to be true, right? You might think I'm exaggerating, but I'm definitely not. I truly believe experiencing gratitude on a daily basis will bring about more positive changes than any other thing you've tried before.

So, are you ready to change your life? I thought so.

Let the miracles begin.

HOW TO DO THE GRATITUDE JAR: GIVE THANKS

. . . .

I created Give THANKS based on my own experience using the Gratitude Jar. Simply Give THANKS for the next thirty days and start your journey to joy, abundance, and miracles.

Give THANKS

Think about what you're grateful for.

Have an open mind.

Allow yourself to feel gratitude.

Note your gratitude.

Keep it in a jar or another special place.

Share it with someone else.

1. **Think about what you're grateful for.** I recommend doing your THANKS at the end of the day, around the same time each night because it's easy to forget if you don't schedule it. Plus, research shows doing a gratitude practice before bed helps you sleep better and wake up more refreshed in the morning.

   Look back on your day and think about everything that happened. Reflect on the people you met, places you visited, and the feelings you experienced. Was there something special that stood out that you're grateful for? Make a note of it.

   Maybe you had a great conversation, or someone did something kind for you. Or you had a positive moment with your children or another loved one. It could also be something really simple like that great brownie you had at lunch (a lot of my gratitudes were food related). Try to come up with as many as you can.

2. **Have an open mind.** Don't judge whatever comes up. Like I said, many of my own gratitudes were about food. Initially, I'd laugh off giving gratitude about something I ate because I thought it wasn't special enough. But when I dug deeper, I realized living in a country where food was abundant was a *huge* blessing and an important gratitude.

   The point is, be open to whatever your heart and your intuition tell you to be thankful for. Giving gratitude for anything, no matter how silly or small you think it may be, is powerful. It's my experience that the best gratitudes usually come in small packages.

3. **Allow yourself to feel gratitude.** Once you've come up with your main gratitude for the day, go a bit deeper into why you chose it. Finish the statement, "I'm thankful because . . ." and provide as many reasons as you can why you're thankful.

   It's a bit like pulling on a thread because once you start thinking of reasons you are grateful for something, more and more things come up. To use the food example, mine would go something like this:

I'm thankful for that turkey sandwich I ate at lunch today. I'm thankful because I was hungry and it satisfied me completely. I'm also thankful because I can always find delicious food to feed myself and my family because I live in a prosperous, developed country. I'm so thankful to God for providing me and my family constant nourishment.

By the end of that exercise, I found my heart was filled with gratitude. Yours will be too. Let gratitude come into your body and enjoy the feeling it gives you. Gratitude is a powerful emotion that instantly washes away stress and tension. Allow yourself to be healed by it.

4. **Note your gratitude.** Write down on a slip of paper what you're grateful for and why. Write "I'm thankful for _____ today because..." and fill it in as completely as possible. There's power from writing something down and making it physical.

   Some of you might be tempted to skip this step because you're feeling so good already—why continue? It's good enough to just think and feel gratitude, right? No. You must write it down. This is a very important step. Putting your gratitude on paper puts it out into the world, which then causes the world to react back positively in response.

5. **Keep it in a jar or another special place.** Your jar can be whatever container you happen to have lying around your house—some people use old coffee cans or mason jars. You could also buy a special container from an antique shop, home décor store, or online if you want something a little more special.

   Decorate it however you wish, but it's important to designate it somehow as *your* Gratitude Jar. I used a simple Post-It note with THANK YOU written on it for mine. You can always ask one of your more crafty friends to help decorate if you don't have the skills yourself. Anything works; you can always start with something you have on hand and then purchase a nicer jar later if you wish.

   When you have your jar ready, put it in a prominent spot of your home to serve as a cue to practice your gratitude each night. Seeing it out with all your slips of gratitude in it is also a great visual reminder of all the good things you have in your life.

6. **Share it with someone else.** There's an old Swedish proverb that says, "Happiness shared is happiness doubled." This is especially true when it comes to gratitude. Sharing your gratitude practice with another person is amazingly powerful, and I sincerely believe it will greatly enhance your results. It certainly did for me.

Will Give THANKS still be effective if you do it on your own? Of course. You'll definitely see transformation if you Give THANKS every night for the next thirty days by yourself. But if you really want to move mountains—share it with someone else.

There have been several studies proving that sharing your happiness with others elevates both your moods and increases your long-term satisfaction with life. These benefits continue long after you've finished sharing. It's also been demonstrated that sharing your happiness is more powerful than simply writing it down. But when happiness is written down *and* shared, both parties receive a huge boost of positivity that continues a considerable amount of time afterwards. It's where the magic lies.

To use a food analogy again: it's like eating a carrot cake without the frosting. While the carrot cake tastes good on its own, it becomes *crazy delicious* with the addition of cream cheese frosting.

Of course it's wonderful if you Give THANKS on your own; gratitude is so powerful that you'll still feel transformation from doing it. But if you share your gratitude practice with someone else—that's when the crazy cream cheese goodness happens. And I know you don't want to miss out on that.

The real power of the Give THANKS practice lies in this step. It's what separates it from any other gratitude practice out there today.

I know you might be uncomfortable asking someone else to do this with you, but tell them about all the benefits that come from doing it: joy, inner peace, abundance, a closer connection with God, and on and on. How could they not want to share it with you?

So here are some ideas for sharing your gratitude practice if you're having a tough time coming up with a partner:

> Do your Gratitude Jar with your child before bedtime like I did.

> Call up your mom, dad, grandma, whomever, and tell them you're going to call them every day for the next thirty days. Keep the Gratitude Jar at your house—then give it to them as a gift for Mother's Day or their birthday.

> Keep the jar by your nightstand and give gratitude with your partner each night before going to bed.

> Put the jar in the middle of the dinner table and share your gratitude during mealtime.

> Start a gratitude group at church.

> Bring the jar with you to book club and share it before you begin your discussion.

> Make it a part of your team meeting at work.

The possibilities are endless, but try to find someone to share your gratitude with. If you prefer to do it alone, like I said, that's okay too. Carrot cake without frosting is still pretty tasty.

But oh, the cream cheese frosting...

VARIATIONS ON THE GRATITUDE JAR

For those of you who want to go even deeper into gratitude, I've included a few more practices. All these practices are simple but incredibly powerful—producing the same transformative results as Give THANKS.

You could do one of these practices at the same time as Give THANKS, or start one right after you've finished your thirty days. Whatever you feel inspired to do.

And obviously, you can do any of these practices, including the Give THANKS, for longer than thirty days if you wish. Once you start practicing gratitude, you might find yourself wanting to continue indefinitely.

That's a good thing.

Gratitude Journal

This is the most popular way to practice gratitude and how Oprah herself does it.

Directions:

1. **Get a journal.** You could buy a blank journal or spiral notebook. There are many beautiful ready-made gratitude journals for sale online or at your local gift or stationary store.

2. **Write down five things you're thankful for at the end of each day.** Every night before bedtime, reflect back on your day and think about five things that happened that you're grateful for. These five things can be anything—from the completely mundane to the really special.

After I finished the Gratitude Jar with Lucas, I wanted to go deeper with my gratitude practice so I made my peace with journaling and started one. I gave the same commitment to do it for thirty days and stuck to it. It helped keep my positive mojo going.

Some nights it was easy to come up with five things; others, not as much. But it was a great way to go even further with gratitude. I continue to alternate between writing in my journal and the Give THANKS practice several times throughout the year.

OPRAH'S GRATITUDE JOURNAL

"So every day for years now, I've written down five things that I'm grateful for," she said. "And you have to write them down because it's very different than just saying, 'Oh, I'm grateful for today.' You have to physically write them down because there's power in the words."

She continued, "Even simple things like fresh flowers or someone opening the door for me. When you wake up in the morning and consciously look for things to be thankful for, you go through the day thinking about the five things that you're going to do in the evening—you are more alive and receptive to the goodness that comes into your life. Because sometimes, it is as simple as somebody holding the door.

"One time it was just two squirrels eating and I thought, *Oh, I better write that down. Nothing else might happen today.*" She laughed.

She continued, "When you allow yourself to feel gratitude in the present moment, in the now, what I promise you is that the spiritual dimension of your life begins to change. It opens up, it expands, and you just grow with it. That is the truth, if I ever spoke the truth in my life. If you want to change your state of being, start to be grateful."

Gratitude Letters

This practice was inspired by a man named John Kra-lik who wrote a book called *A Simple Act of Gratitude: How Learning to Say Thank You Changed My Life*. John wrote a thank-you note every day over the course of a year and documented his experience in a book. In a nutshell, it changed his life.

Directions:

1. **Write a thank-you note to someone every day for the next thirty days.** Instructions for how to write a good thank-you note are included below.

How to Write a Good Thank-You Note :

Use the simple thank-you letter template: Who, What, When.

WHO
Write down a list of everyone you need to thank. Think of people who have made a positive impact on you or just did something nice for you one day. Try to think of as many people as you can: friends, family, coworkers, service workers, anyone that you encounter during any given day that has touched you in some way. You can add

to your list as you go along, since I guarantee once you start practicing this that you'll start noticing kind acts from other people more often.

WHAT
Here's a breakdown of a good thank-you note along with a few sample phrases to get you started (and finished):

1. **Greeting.** Don't forget to make sure you're using the correct form and spelling of the person's name as well as anyone else's name mentioned in the note.

   Dear Aunt Sharon and Uncle Bob,

2. **Express your thanks.** Begin with the two most important words: *Thank you.*

   Thank you so much for . . . I'm so grateful you were there when . . .

   a. **Add specific details.** Tell them how their actions or gifts affected you, even if it was something simple like holding open the door for you.

   Your friendship means so much to me. I appreciate that whenever I call, you're always there to listen.

The money you gave will help pay for my college and fulfill my dreams of becoming a veterinarian.

3. **Look ahead.** Mention the next time you might see them, or just let them know you're thinking of them.

   I look forward to seeing you at our next book club meeting.

4. **Restate your thanks.** Add details to thank them in a different way.

   Again, thank you for your generosity. I'm so excited about college. I'll let you know all about it when I get settled.

   We felt so blessed that you made the trip to be with us on our wedding day. We can't wait to see you again soon!

5. **End with your regards.** "Sincerely" and "Best" are always safe, but for closer relationships, you might choose a warmer option.

   With love,

   Many thanks,

JOHN KRALIK'S THANK-YOU NOTES

The following are a sampling of thank-you notes that John Kralik wrote over the course of the year. One was written to his best friend Bob, who helped him through a crisis, and another to his daughter. The last was to the Starbucks guy, which I thought was sweet and funny.

Dear Bob,

Thank you so much for taking me to one of my favorite places for lunch. It felt like my birthday. Thanks for all the times you've spent talking through my recent issues, and being there in my moments of crisis. Thank you too for having the courage to share with me the difficulties that you have had—it reminds me that others face greater challenges and are able to summon far greater courage than is asked of me. I was moved by your confidence that I would make it. By listening and caring, you have made a tremendous difference in my life.

Sincerely,

John

My daughter,

Thank you for being cheerful and happy when I pick you up in the evening. Sometimes I don't have a very fun day, but when I see you and we talk about things and have fun, I feel better. Thank you for being the best daughter ever.

Love,
Dad

Scott (the Starbucks guy),

Thank you for taking the time to greet me each morning in a friendly way. It is also so wonderful to me that you took the time to remember my name. In this day and age, few people make this effort, and fewer still do it in a way that feels sincere. You do both. It really makes a difference to me each day.

Best,
John

John remarks that the notes should be handwritten and not emailed. "The thank-you notes that came to me [in reply] reinforced my conviction that handwriting is important and special, that it forces concentration on the task. I continue to believe the best notes are handwritten. A handwritten note just feels like sincere gratitude."

Gratitude Meditation

My mentor, Maleah Jacobs, is a big believer in the benefits of meditating daily. It calms the mind, increases creativity and intuition, improves health, and just makes you feel good. Maleah herself meditates several hours each day. She considers it an essential ingredient to her success as a healer and an important part of her spiritual foundation along with her daily gratitude practice.

There has been a wealth of research into the benefits of having a regular meditation practice; by including gratitude, you'll find your results are even more rewarding. As a way to experience the best of both worlds, I created the following guided gratitude meditation. I've used it many times to enhance my own gratitude practice, and it has helped me tremendously.

This is a great meditation to do at the beginning of the day, or very end. Turn off your phone and free yourself of interruptions. Either sit or lie down, whatever is most comfortable. Now close your eyes.

Take a long, slow, deep breath in and slowly exhale. Feel any tension melting away as you gradually relax deeper with each breath.

Take another long, slow, deep breath in and exhale. Feel yourself drifting into a state of deep relaxation.

Continue to breathe slowly and gently as you bring

your awareness to the top of your head. Picture a warm, loving light spreading from the top of your head down to your toes. Feel your muscles relax as the light washes over you, surrounding and protecting you. Take a few more deep breaths and relax deeply.

In this safe, relaxed state, reflect on all the things you're grateful for: loved ones, breath in your lungs, sunshine, fresh air, the tasty dinner you had that evening, a nice compliment from a coworker—whatever comes to mind.

As each gratitude appears, visualize yourself saying the words *thank you* to each. Picture the person you're grateful for standing in front of you, and tell them how grateful you are for them and why. Try to make the image and feeling as real as you can. Taste the delicious apple you ate for lunch, and say thank you to it. If you're having a difficult time coming up with gratitudes, ask God to reveal them to you. God will.

Allow the feeling of deep gratitude to come into your body. Notice where in your body the feeling is. Take a few deep breaths and allow this feeling to expand. Enjoy the pleasant feeling gratitude gives you, and feel it washing away your tension and negativity. You can remain in this relaxed state as long as you like.

When you're ready, end your gratitude meditation with the following affirmation: *Thank you for the many blessings I have been bestowed with. May these blessings multiply* as I continue to notice and give thanks for them. Thank you, God. Amen.

Wiggle your toes and fingers, open your eyes, and give yourself a few moments to adjust. Bring that feeling of gratitude with you as you go through your day or drift off to sleep.

MALEAH JACOBS ON GRATITUDE: PRIMING THE PUMP

I grew up reading, then watching, *Little House on the Prairie*. When Laura Ingalls would go to the well, she would prime the pump. After pumping the well handle for water several times, I noticed what happened. Or rather what didn't happen, at least not right away.

Nothing came out of the pump.

She saw no tangible results at first. No water. However, after several times, the water would begin to flow. This was a small but significant act of faith. She knew after priming the pump that the water would soon begin to flow freely and easily. And with consistency, the water would continue to flow, and flow, and flow.

When we apply this to gratitude, we experience the same results with grander outcomes. Things flow easily and we realize there is more than enough. There is no scarcity. No lack. No limitation. Only our false belief in any idea of scarcity. The truth is that there is an abundance and plenty for all. But this realization only comes from practicing gratitude consistently.

That's why it is called a spiritual *practice*.

Simple gratitude practices can be incorporated easily, and I find myself using a handful of them every day. When I let up on the consistency, it shows. My life feels slightly off-kilter. That feeling is useful information and tells me to go back to basics and practice gratitude for all the good, and even what feels like (at the time) the not-so-good, experiences. They all prove useful. When paired with time, it equals perspective, and perspective is a powerful thing because it leads to gratitude.

You may not feel the full benefits of your gratitude practice at first, but in due time they will reveal themselves. Before you know it, there will be dozens, if not hundreds, of people, places, and things you will feel immensely grateful for in your life.

Never underestimate your own strength. We humans are resilient, strong creatures, able to bounce back from the brink time and again. We are not at the mercy of externals. Ever. It's only our thoughts that have us feeling like rudderless ships.

Our consciousness is where it's at. What we put our attention to increases. What we appreciate, appreciates. The six inches between our ears are the most powerful part of the human body. I invite you to entertain the idea of allowing your life to get easier by focusing on all the many things you are grateful for in your life. Because that is what you will get more of in your life. And you'll feel better. And better.

And better ... is better.

I know I've done my life the hard way, and if you're reading this book, you probably have too. You're not alone. Welcome to the human condition. But now, it is time for an easier way. Or you wouldn't have this book in your hands. Divine Timing and all.

Go for good, and all that's not the truth of you will fall away.

There is a huge ripple effect each of us has on this planet. When working with clients, or even chatting with chums, I have no idea what will come of it. Frequently, I learn later of some kind of support that was provided and how it has affected someone. Like Josie.

Now this book is out in the world touching lives that I will know nothing about. Those lives will go on to touch the lives of others. And so on. And on it goes.

You are powerful. And we need you to be. The planet needs all of us to show up and show out. To claim our birthright. The simple act of practicing gratitude, consistently, is your invitation to a new life. Accepting the invitation is now up to you.

Have faith in priming your own gratitude pump and most of all ... Thank you.

Maleah Jacobs

AFTER GRATITUDE: ONE YEAR LATER

"I don't have to chase extraordinary moments to find happiness—it's right in front of me if I'm paying attention and practicing gratitude."

—Brené Brown

It's been a little over a year since the Gratitude Jar first came into my life, and as I look back at what's happened over the course of this past year I can honestly say, without question, it's been the most extraordinary period of my life.

Here I sit at my computer, writing, looking out the window, reflecting on everything that's happened—and the view I see is completely different from the one I saw a year ago. Yes, I now see the world with new eyes, but also the view itself is actually physically different; we moved out of our little rambler into our dream home about six months after Lucas and I said our first thank-yous together.

A total and complete dream home. The never-thought-we-could-afford-this-on-our-income home.

We'd been trying unsuccessfully to move into a new home for years but never had enough money for a down payment because we couldn't sell our house without breaking the bank. Our neighborhood was one of the hardest hit by the housing crash; our house was worth way less than we paid for it, and we were probably never going to sell it for any kind of profit in our lifetime.

We'd also resigned ourselves to the fact the house we would eventually move into would be a major fixer-upper because of how expensive the homes were in the nicer neighborhoods we wanted to move into. The only homes for sale in our price range in those areas were basically about to be condemned.

But through a series of what I can only describe as miraculous events, we found and moved into an amazing home, completely perfect for us, in one of the nicest neighborhoods of the Twin Cities. This was a miracle I never dreamt possible a year ago, but now, miracles seem to follow me wherever I go.

☙ Our house situation was just one of the many amazing things that happened this past year; there have been many others. I'm still sober, I lost the twenty extra pounds of baby weight I'd been lugging around (by changing thoughts of hating my body to finding reasons to be thankful for it), I continue to work in a job I love with enough money to live comfortably, and my relationships with everyone, especially those within my immediate family, have greatly improved.

I feel happy, content, and peaceful (I still have my moments, of course). But the smile on my face these days is completely and totally 100 percent sincere. It feels really good to be alive.

I never would have said that before practicing gratitude.

A year ago, before the Gratitude Jar, I was drunk and miserable, contemplating how my family would be better off without me. I had no purpose. I didn't know how to escape the black hole I'd fallen into. Thankfully, God, Maleah, and the Gratitude Jar with Lucas pulled me out of the darkness into the light.

☞ I've thought a lot about why this seemingly simple thing, this little jar, caused such a huge shift in my way of thinking. I realized the answer was obvious: Gratitude made me realize everything I ever needed was already right there in front of me. And I finally, truly, enjoyed it.

The default setting of my brain was negativity and a constant, obsessive search for "that thing" to make me feel better. Nothing ever worked, and I continued to rage on trying to find it. The Buddha said this desire to want for things that ultimately never satisfy is the cause of human suffering. I agree with him completely; it was definitely the cause of my own. I was never satisfied, and it made me miserable.

But Buddha also said the way to be free of this suffering was to live in and find peace in the present moment. To end the constant search for *something* to fill the void and instead, just be happy with wherever you were *right now.*

I didn't know how to do that until I discovered gratitude.

Gratitude forced me to live in the present and look at my life *as it was* and appreciate all that was there. I quit thinking about all the things I "needed" to make me happy—being thinner, richer, whatever else—and instead focused on everything I already had. When I finally did that, I realized everything I ever needed was right there in front of me waiting for me to notice and appreciate it.

Now, I notice everything.

And I have to say, things are pretty damn good.

Now, the default setting of my brain is gratitude. As I go through the day I have hundreds of little "gratitude moments." Most of them are about seemingly mundane things like trees, water, my family, food—but I have the awareness now that these simple little things are downright extraordinary because I *see* them through the eyes of gratitude.

Thanks to a simple jar, I finally see life as it really is: A miracle.

掗 Hey, God! It's me again. What's new? So, you really outdid yourself this time. I certainly didn't expect all this. Wow! Thank you.

But most of all, thank you for teaching me how to say thank you. I didn't realize saying thanks would be the thing to lead me to my highest purpose and to you, but obviously you knew what you were doing. As you always do. Thank you for showing me the way.

I'll never lose it again.

Amen.

RESOURCES &
SUGGESTED READING:

The Attitude of Gratitude, a Pair of Parables, www.tribe.net

Thanks! How the New Science of Gratitude Can Make You Happier, Robert Emmons, August 6, 2007, Houghton Mifflin Harcourt.

Oprah's Lifeclass: Oprah's Gratitude Journal, www.oprah.com

A Simple Act of Gratitude: How Learning to Say Thank You Changed My Life, John Kralik, December 27, 2011, Hyperion.

On a Personal Note: Thank You, www.hallmark.com

Holy Bible, English Standard Version.

The Gifts of Imperfection: Let Go of Who You Think You're Supposed to Be and Embrace Who You Are, Brené Brown, Hazelden, August 27, 2010.

One Thousand Gifts: A Dare to Live Fully Right Where You Are, Ann Voskamp, Zondervan, 19th Edition, January 26, 2011.

**For more information about Maleah Jacobs,
visit: www.MaleahJacobs.com**

AN INVITATION...

For more miracles, visit me at:

josierobinson.com

DEDICATION

I could never have written a book about gratitude had it not been for all the incredible people that touched my life along the way. To them, and to those of you who just finished reading this book, *thank you.*